5/11

HIP-HOP

Alicia Keys
Ashanti
Beyoncé
Black Eyed Peas
Busta Rhymes
Chris Brown
Christina Aguilera
Ciara
Cypress Hill
Daddy Yankee
DMX
Don Omar
Dr. Dre
Eminem
Fat Joe
50 Cent
The Game
Hip-Hop: A Short History
Hip-Hop Around the World
Ice Cube
Ivy Queen
Jay-Z
Jennifer Lopez
Juelz Santana
Kanye West

Lil Wayne
LL Cool J
Lloyd Banks
Ludacris
Mariah Carey
Mary J. Blige
Missy Elliot
Nas
Nelly
Notorious B.I.G.
OutKast
Pharrell Williams
Pitbull
Queen Latifah
Reverend Run (of Run DMC)
Sean "Diddy" Combs
Snoop Dogg
T.I.
Tupac
Usher
Will Smith
Wu-Tang Clan
Xzibit
Young Jeezy
Yung Joc

Young Jeezy may be young, but he has become a big name on the hip-hop scene. And it's likely he'll be around for some time to come.

Young Jeezy

Nat Cotts

Mason Crest Publishers

Young Jeezy

Produced by Harding House Publishing Service, Inc.
201 Harding Avenue, Vestal, NY 13850.

MASON CREST PUBLISHERS INC.
370 Reed Road
Broomall, Pennsylvania 19008
(866)MCP-BOOK (toll free)
www.masoncrest.com

Printed in the United States of America

First Printing

9 8 7 6 5 4 3 2 1

Library of Congress Cataloging-in-Publication Data

Cotts, Nat.
  Young Jeezy / Nat Cotts.
      p. cm. — (Hip-hop)
  Includes index.
  ISBN 978-1-4222-0306-4
  ISBN: 978-1-4222-0077-3 (series)
  1. Young Jeezy—Juvenile literature. 2. Rap musicians—United States—Biography—Juvenile literature. I. Title.
  ML3930.Y68C68 2008
  782.421649092—dc22
                              2007032957

Publisher's notes:
• All quotations in this book come from original sources and contain the spelling and grammatical inconsistencies of the original text.

• The Web sites mentioned in this book were active at the time of publication. The publisher is not responsible for Web sites that have changed their addresses or discontinued operation since the date of publication. The publisher will review and update the Web site addresses each time the book is reprinted.

DISCLAIMER: The following story has been thoroughly researched, and to the best of our knowledge, represents a true story. While every possible effort has been made to ensure accuracy, the publisher will not assume liability for damages caused by inaccuracies in the data, and makes no warranty on the accuracy of the information contained herein. This story has not been authorized nor endorsed by Young Jeezy.

Contents

Hip-Hop Time Line   6

1 The King of New York   9

2 A Southern Boy   15

3 Acting Thug   27

4 Protecting His Neck   35

5 Katrina   45

Chronology   56

Accomplishments and Awards   58

Further Reading/Internet Resources   59

Glossary   61

Index   62

About the Author   64

Picture Credits   64

Hip-Hop Time Line

1976 Grandmaster Flash and the Furious Five emerge as one of the first battlers and freestylers.

1984 The track "Roxanne Roxanne" sparks the first diss war.

1970s DJ Kool Herc pioneers the use of breaks, isolations, and repeats using two turn-tables.

1988 Hip-hop record sales reach 100 million annually.

1982 Afrika Bambaataa tours Europe in another hip-hop first.

1970s Grafitti artist Vic begins tagging on New York subways.

1980 Rapper Kurtis Blow sells a million records and makes the first nationwide TV appearance for a hip-hop artist.

1985 The film *Krush Groove*, about the rise of Def Jam Records, is released.

1970   1980

1970s The central elements of the hip-hop culture begin to emerge in the Bronx, New York City.

1983 Ice-T releases his first singles, marking the earliest examples of gangsta rap.

1986 Run DMC cover Aerosmith's "Walk this Way" and appear on the cover of *Rolling Stone*.

1979 "Rapper's Delight," by The Sugarhill Gang, goes gold.

1984 *Graffitti Rock*, the first hip-hop television program, premieres.

1974 Afrika Bambaataa organizes the Universal Zulu Nation.

1988 MTV premieres *Yo! MTV Raps*.

1981 Grandmaster Flash and the Furious Five release *Adventures on the Wheels of Steel*.

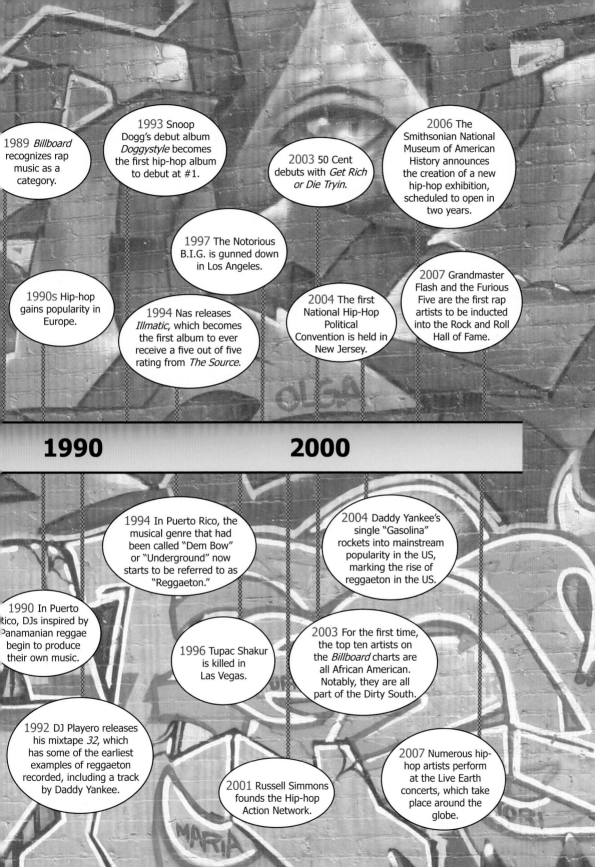

1989 *Billboard* recognizes rap music as a category.

1993 Snoop Dogg's debut album *Doggystyle* becomes the first hip-hop album to debut at #1.

2003 50 Cent debuts with *Get Rich or Die Tryin.*

2006 The Smithsonian National Museum of American History announces the creation of a new hip-hop exhibition, scheduled to open in two years.

1997 The Notorious B.I.G. is gunned down in Los Angeles.

1990s Hip-hop gains popularity in Europe.

1994 Nas releases *Illmatic*, which becomes the first album to ever receive a five out of five rating from *The Source*.

2004 The first National Hip-Hop Political Convention is held in New Jersey.

2007 Grandmaster Flash and the Furious Five are the first rap artists to be inducted into the Rock and Roll Hall of Fame.

1990

2000

1994 In Puerto Rico, the musical genre that had been called "Dem Bow" or "Underground" now starts to be referred to as "Reggaeton."

2004 Daddy Yankee's single "Gasolina" rockets into mainstream popularity in the US, marking the rise of reggaeton in the US.

1990 In Puerto Rico, DJs inspired by Panamanian reggae begin to produce their own music.

1996 Tupac Shakur is killed in Las Vegas.

2003 For the first time, the top ten artists on the *Billboard* charts are all African American. Notably, they are all part of the Dirty South.

1992 DJ Playero releases his mixtape *32*, which has some of the earliest examples of reggaeton recorded, including a track by Daddy Yankee.

2001 Russell Simmons founds the Hip-hop Action Network.

2007 Numerous hip-hop artists perform at the Live Earth concerts, which take place around the globe.

XXL calls him New York's King of Hip-Hop. That's high praise for a young guy from Georgia. But Young Jeezy has proved that he's worthy of the title.

The King of New York

Young Jeezy had had many good moments in his career by the time the spring of 2006 rolled around. He was already one of the biggest names in hip-hop, having sold more than two and a half million copies of his third album, *Thug Motivation 101*, with six singles getting heavy airtime on radios worldwide, and multiple videos appearing frequently on MTV and BET. For fans of Southern **rap**, he was a living legend, right up there with Lil Jon and T.I. There didn't seem to be any room for him to go higher. He could certainly win an award or two, perhaps a Grammy, but after the kind of success he was having, those would have been mere formalities.

And yet he did go higher, and he did it in a way that turned the old order of hip-hop upside down.

Ruling New York

In 2006, one of the biggest magazines in hip-hop, *XXL*, crowned Jeezy New York's King of Hip-Hop, marking him as the most popular and influential rapper currently on the cultural radar of the city's inhabitants. According to the magazine, Young Jeezy had the whole city in the palm of his hand.

Anyone who knows much about hip-hop—and especially anyone as deep into hip-hop as the journalists who make their bread and butter writing about the music—knows there is no higher title for a rapper than "King of New York." After all, New York is the place where hip-hop was born. It was there in the Bronx that DJ Kool Herc introduced the world to the art of DJing at his famed rec-room parties. Since then, hip-hop has spread from New York. During the early nineties, N.W.A, Compton, and the West Coast had the nation's attention, and then Southern rap introduced its own kind of sound, but New York's hip-hop voice has always remained loud and strong.

The rappers who had held the royal title before Jeezy were, like Jay-Z and Nas, among the most admired stars in hip-hop's galaxy—or at least, like Notorious B.I.G., they stood out from all the others! But unlike the others, Young Jeezy wasn't from anywhere near New York. He wasn't even from the East Coast. In a hip-hop world where rappers are often judged simply by the location of their birth, Young Jeezy was the outsider claiming the insider's crown. He was a rapper from Atlanta, from the heart of the Dirty South.

Southern Hip-Hop

Southern hip-hop got its start when young rappers from cities like Houston, Dallas, Atlanta, and Memphis began to imitate the music that came pounding out from the Bronx in the mid-seventies. The South had all the elements of a thriving hip-hop

Young Jeezy's crown as king has been previously worn by some of the biggest names in the history of hip-hop. One of them was Jay-Z, a hip-hop icon.

scene, with **mixtapes** from Southern rappers multiplying by the minute and turning up even in the streets of the Bronx and Compton, California.

But the rappers up North and in the West looked down their noses at the South's hip-hop offerings. As the seventies became the eighties, and the West Coast began to challenge the East for dominance, laying the roots for the rivalry that some claim killed rappers Tupac Shakur and Biggie Smalls, there just wasn't room in their world for the South's version

Though East Coast and West Coast rap might be better known, the South has a claim to one of the most popular forms—Dirty South rap. Cities like Atlanta have proved to be a fertile launching ground for Dirty South rappers like Young Jeezy.

of hip-hop. The two coasts at least respected the talent of the other, in the way that a Red Sox fan respects the talent of the players on the Yankees. Rappers and fans from one coast could be expected to slam each other any chance they got, but they didn't just dismiss them having no talent.

Southern hip-hop, though, found itself being dismissed by both coasts as being crude and completely without talent. Southern rap was like the kid brother no one took seriously. A few artists from the South, such as the Geto Boys from Houston, were able to reach nationwide success, but on the whole, the South would not "grow up" until the late nineties.

Atlanta, the capital of the state of Georgia and home to the largest urban African American population in the Southern United States, blossomed into a major hip-hop city. Soon, thanks to artists like Lil Wayne and Missy Elliott, Southern rap was taking its place beside both East Coast hip-hop and the West Coast version. The kid brother had grown up!

Hip-hop purists, however, weren't ready to accept the South's rap. Some said it wasn't "real" hip-hop; other critics insisted that Southern rap was "killing" hip-hop. True, just as West Coast hip-hop differed from the East Coast, Southern hip-hop was different from both; where the "classic" hip-hop from both coasts emphasized sharp rhymes and storytelling over the beat, Southern hip-hop was more about the beat itself. Critics called it "dumbed-down" hip-hop.

So for a Southern rapper like Young Jeezy to be called the "King of New York" was a triumph for the entire South. But his success had only just begun.

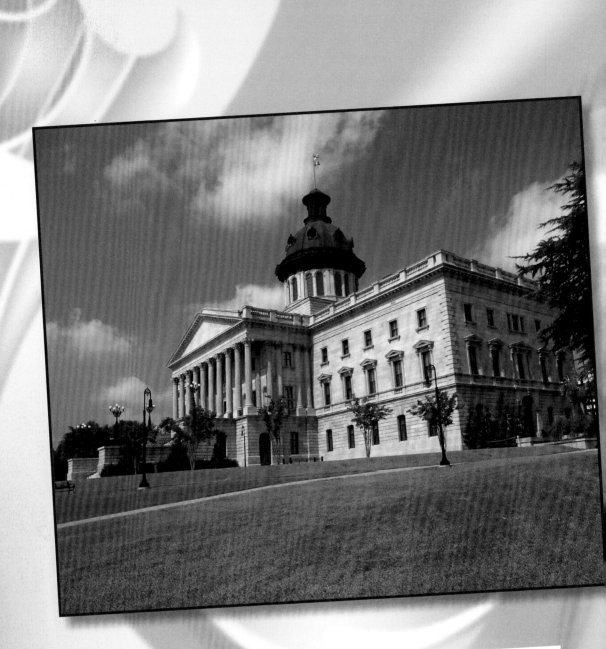

Jay Jenkins, whom the world would one day know better as Young Jeezy, was born in Columbia, South Carolina. But he and his family didn't live there for long.

A Southern Boy

Jay Jenkins was born on September 28, 1979, in the city of Columbia, South Carolina. He had several siblings, among them a younger brother. His father was not around, and his mother raised the family. Other than that, all Jeezy has ever said about his childhood was that it was "empty." Odds are, it was the sort of life faced by many black children living in poverty throughout the United States: a single-parent family, living in a bad neighborhood, stuck in a life without many of the opportunities middle- and upper- class children take for granted.

Jay and his family moved from Columbia soon after his birth, crossing the southern border of South Carolina and ending up in the city of Macon, Georgia, a suburb of the great city of Atlanta. The greater metropolitan area of which Atlanta is the heart is equal to New York and Los Angeles as a center for African American **culture**, and Jay Jenkins came on the scene just in time for the rise of Southern rap and hip-hop. Labels like Cash Money and No Limit Records were born in the early nineties, just as Jay's age reached the double digits, a time when he was ripe and ready to soak in all the new hip-hop rhythms flowing around him. He grew up hearing the sounds of Notorious B.I.G., Tupac Shakur, and Wu-Tang Clan—but also the multitude of Southern rappers who were flowering, even though they were still below the hip-hop nation's radar.

Jay grew up on the streets. His interviews make clear that as he grew older, his life was less than squeaky clean: he hung out with gang members and used and dealt illegal drugs. But all that would change. Jay Jenkins put that life aside, turned to music, and became Lil' J.

Musical Beginnings

As a musician, Lil' J made it clear that he was a "hustler," willing to work as hard as it took to achieve success, no matter what stood in his way. Later, when he changed his identity yet again to "Young Jeezy," this philosophy still defined his entire career. He told the *Village Voice*:

> *"I'm a hustler, and I wouldn't never say what my hustle was because that ain't for everybody to know. But I got 25 years of this . . . in me; what else am I going to talk about? . . . I'm a hustler; that's what I been doing all my life. . . . So I ask you: you think I'm a get tired of talking about it or run out of [stuff] to say? Never. That's what I am. It's even better because maybe now I'll have more positive things to talk about and more people will want to hear. I can talk about the good and the bad now instead of just being about the bad."*

Sometimes when you're poor you'll do almost anything to earn some money. Some career choices—like selling drugs—can make a bad situation worse.

For Jeezy, hustling and rapping go together. And no matter what he's doing, he works hard at it.

He put out his first album, *Thuggin Under the Influence*, independently, under his own label, Corporate Thugz Entertainment. Clearly, although Jeezy had moved from drug dealing to music making, his mind was still back on the streets! The album came out in late 2001 to mixed reviews. Some people liked the *tracks*; others felt that the independent, low-

Young Jeezy decided to give up his life as a hustler. He wanted something better than life on the streets, and he knew he could get it through music.

budget production methods were way too obvious, with cheap beats and raps that struggled to stay on time with the song. The album, despite its flaws, still sold a respectable number of copies for an independent production—but you couldn't say it turned Jeezy into an overnight success. In keeping with his work ethic, however, that didn't slow him down.

By 2003, he was back, with a new album and a new name. Now calling himself Young Jeezy, he produced another independent album, *Come Shop wit Me*, a two-disc set that contained both new material and a revamping of his earlier album. Despite all the problems of distribution and advertising that independent records face, *Come Shop wit Me* racked up a surprising 50,000 in sales worldwide. Granted, this didn't make the album a smash hit, nor was Jeezy taking his place yet among the great hip-hop stars. However, the album gave Jeezy a foundation on which to build, both with fans and, more important, with music industry insiders.

Inside the Game

The album gave him **credibility**, or "cred." As a result, Young Jeezy was able to sign with a top-of-the-line label, Bad Boy Records, and join the Boyz n Da Hood group. No longer a hustling outsider, he was now inside the game, playing with the big boys. With the release of Boyz n Da Hood's self-titled album in 2005, Jeezy found himself well on his way to being a hip-hop star. The album reached #5 on the coveted *Billboard* 200 chart, making it a smash success.

Young Jeezy's future was looking bright, but he still wasn't ready to sit back and enjoy the ride. Even while he was working on the album with Boyz n Da Hood, he was cutting another one of his own. His third solo album—his first on a major record label—was titled *Let's Get It: Thug Motivation 101*.

The new album outsold *Come Shop wit Me* three times over in the first week alone. Eventually it sold 1.7 million copies in the United States and reached 2.5 million worldwide. Young Jeezy's victory made people take notice of the young artist. And it gave Young Jeezy the confidence he needed to succeed as a full-blown hip-hop star on his own, not tied down to a four-member group.

Going It Solo

By the middle of October 2005, Young Jeezy had broken away from Boyz n Da Hood. During interviews, he made it clear he had always considered himself a solo artist. A year later, in December of 2006, he came out with another album, *The Inspiration*. In six months, the new album sold a million copies in the United States. Young Jeezy was not only a successful rapper now; he was one of the greatest in the business.

The Snowman

Like many other hip-hop stars, Young Jeezy used his new success—and the money that came with it—to become an **entrepreneur**. Successful rappers, both young and old, have a habit of hustling hard and in many directions. They use the money they've made for themselves with music to fund business ventures. Lots of times, successful artists use their star power and street cred to sell designer clothing with their names on it. This was the route Young Jeezy took as well. As soon as his first album made him a hip-hop sensation, back in 2005, Young Jeezy began putting out clothes to take advantage of his music success.

The success of a hip-hop clothing line always depends on the rapper who sells it, so Jeezy made sure his first offering was something that could be clearly identified with him. A nickname that he had proudly kept throughout his career was "The Snowman"; for his clothing line, he made himself a logo based on this name: a classic white snowman sporting a very hip-hop snarl, complete with a strong line for a mouth and angry eyebrows.

So when is a snowman not a snowman? When it's a symbol for dealing cocaine. Kids loved Young Jeezy's Snowman t-shirts, but savvy school principals didn't.

The first item of clothing Young Jeezy picked to bear the Snowman was a t-shirt. In this version, the snowman, out on the front of the shirt over the pecs, was about four inches high and glittered like diamonds. It was a good-looking shirt that proved to be popular with Young Jeezy's new fans. Across the country, middle-schoolers and high-schoolers were soon sporting the snowman.

That was a good thing, right? Well, as it turned out, most of them couldn't wear the shirts in school. Many principals and teachers, at least those who had enough street sense to know who the Snowman was, didn't want their students wearing the shirts. Young Jeezy made no secret of the fact that before he wised up and devoted himself to the hip-hop business, he had dealt cocaine. In the style of the gangsta rap hip-hop world, he flaunted his past as a way to keep up his street reputation, making sure he threw his "Snowman" nickname around as much as possible. Snow is slang for cocaine, and a snowman, on the street, is a dealer. That's why the school administrators and teachers didn't like the shirts!

By wearing the shirts, school personnel felt, kids were saying they supported the cocaine business. Most of the kids wearing the shirts probably didn't think of it that way. They were just wearing Snowman shirts because they were cool.

Young Jeezy, meanwhile, probably hadn't expected such a big stir over a shirt. Although he certainly doesn't deny that "snowman" is street slang for "cocaine dealer", he also makes it clear that the logo is more about him than cocaine. According to Jeezy, if you take the shirt to mean anything, you should take it to mean that the person wearing it is "feeling gangsta." For Jeezy, and for many others in the hip-hop world, "gangsta" is about a culture, an attitude, and a style. Many others, however, still disapprove; they say that this culture is associated with violence, that the attitude is often rude and disrespectful, and that no style is worth being associated with such a negative outlook.

U.S.D.A.

Young Jeezy has also made moves to expand his brand even further. In 2006, he expanded his clothing line beyond t-shirts, a move that puts him alongside industry *moguls* like P Diddy and Jay-Z, although, according to Young Jeezy, his clothing is far more authentic gangsta then theirs! Jeezy plans to expand his brand to everything from shoes to workout gear, all stamped with his 8732 symbol.

So why did Jeezy choose those numerals for his logo? The numbers, when transposed into letters as you would on a touch-tone phone, stand for "U.S.D.A."—the United Streets of Dope-boys of America—which is what Young Jeezy originally wanted to call the clothing line. However, the name was already taken, by the United States Department of Agriculture no less, the government organization responsible for overseeing everything from the use of pesticides on crops in the United States to the specialty diets that children and pregnant women require. As Young Jeezy found out, the government doesn't like having its names and acronyms imitated, at least when someone is going to make a profit from it. So, Jeezy used the numbers instead.

Jeezy also produced a mixtape with the same acronym: *Young Jeezy Presents U.S.D.A.* Two other rappers join him on the tape—Blood Raw and Sick Pulla, both Southern rappers with styles similar to Jeezy's. The tape is a lot like a motivational seminar for street kids. According to Christopher Catania of PopMatter.com:

> *"Beyond the club-banging tracks, it's in this motivational context that Young Jeezy's often dry and blatant lyrics and epic anthems make a lot more sense, making him stand out among the other Southern rappers. Having a clear picture of his audience in mind helps you to understand that Young Jeezy understands that*

the rap game is a business and when he says in the liner notes that, 'at the end of the day red and blue make green so let go get it!!' he really means it."

Some may wonder if Young Jeezy is really the sort of role model who should be advising young adults. Others say he's exactly the sort of role model that kids will pay attention to.

Hip-hop stars and clothing lines seem to go together, and Young Jeezy is no exception. He's expanding his clothing line beyond the infamous Snowman t-shirts.

After all, he knows what he's talking about. One young person posted on the *Village Voice*'s Web site how he feels about Jeezy and his music:

> *"I feel whats Jeezy is talking about because I was kinda like him when I was growing up in the streets hustling to feed myself and feed my family. And I try to be my self to the fullest. . . . Now I'm 15 years old, grinding hard and guess what I'm listening to? Thug Motivation!"*

You got to say this much for Young Jeezy: he's got cred!

Over the years, hip-hop and violence have been closely associated. Young Jeezy makes sure to play up his former gangsta life, though some question just how gangsta it really was.

Acting Thug

One thing that's always hard to tell in hip-hop is how much a particular rapper's gangster image is true to life, and how much is front and flash. Part of succeeding in the hip-hop business is having a image and a story—living a life outside the law before you became legit by getting in front of the microphone and rapping for money and fame.

Building an Image

One of the most convincing types of gangsta image is built on having been shot. After all, really, is there any way to show how tough you are than to have come back from having had a few holes punched in you? Or better yet, to have led the sort of life where someone would *want* to shoot you in the first place? 50 Cent is probably the most famous example of a hip-hop star who uses his real-life run-ins with a bullet to get street cred, but there are plenty of other rappers besides him who have taken a bullet. In fact, there are so many people in the business with that story that it's even become a bit of a joke; a *Sopranos* episode featured a would-be rapper who tried to pay Tony to shoot him to give him street cred.

Although Young Jeezy can't boast that he's ever been shot, he can rap about his past as a gangsta instead. He's careful to always play up the gangsta lifestyle he once lived as much as possible. Of course, there's some question as to how much of a gangster he really was, and just how deeply he was into the cocaine trade—but really, who wants to quibble about details like that? Clearly, Jeezy knows the life he raps about.

When *XXL* magazine interviewed Jeezy, he said, "I know I got love for this music 'cause it's a hustle." *XXL* added:

> *"It's a hustle Jeezy has studied well. In today's street-cred obsessed rap market, an artist's lifestyle is often more important than his talent. (Think DMX or Jim Jones.) It's safe to say that many of Jeezy's fans are more intrigued by the man than the music. As another popular aphorism would put it: He gets it how he lives. 'Tupac was one of the realest,' says Jeezy. 'And everybody bought his records 'cause he was that type of dude. I want to be in that position. Not a position where I might have a hot song and then three months later you don't know who I am. I'd rather be in the hearts and minds instead of on the shelves.'"*

Drugs and Violence

Just how much he should be glorifying street life is another question, and one that Young Jeezy would probably brush off. However, Young Jeezy and other rappers like him—"coke rappers" who perform "crack rap"—are **controversial** figures. High school principals and education watchdogs are not the

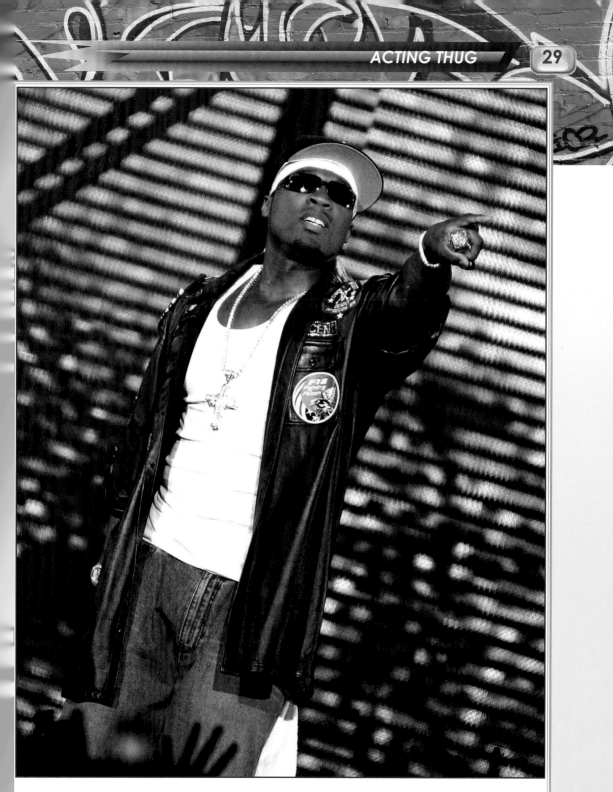

Street cred is important to a hip-hop artist's image. If you're a gang-sta rapper, the street cred is usually related to run-ins with violence. Based on that, 50 Cent has more street cred than most.

only ones who disapprove of Jeezy's lyrics and life. Even many in the hip-hop world itself—people like hip-hop mogul Russell Simmons—condemn Jeezy and other gangsta rappers for glorifying drugs and gang violence, for promoting misogyny (the hatred of women), and for seeming to actively encourage some of the many problems that plague urban communities.

Critics have found much to complain about in hip-hop. One of their biggest complaints is how some rap lyrics seem to glorify violence against and the mistreatment of women.

Many people hold crack (a cheaper form of cocaine) responsible for the decline of inner cities. Crack not only destroys lives through addiction but also through the crime it breeds: addicts often turn to crime as a means to get money for a fix, while drug dealers run a violent business. Homicide is the leading cause of death for young black males between the ages of fifteen and thirty-four; the vast majority of these murders are committed with firearms.

Young Jeezy's critics say his raps glorify this destructive lifestyle—and by doing so, Jeezy is making a buck off the life-and-death circumstances many African Americans face every day, sometimes not of their own doing. His raps, say these critics, propel the cycle of violence to continue—and even get worse—by glorifying it, encouraging youth to become drug dealers and gangsters themselves. Some even say that Young Jeezy and rappers like him give all of black America a bad name.

However, Young Jeezy has supporters as well. They say that while the sort of life Jeezy rhymes about may be ugly, nasty, and bad, it is still reality. Young Jeezy, they say, is simply representing life as it is on the street—and anyone who criticizes him for that just doesn't know what it's really like out there in the real world. Maybe the truth hurts, but no good comes from hiding it out of sight!

Young Jeezy, meanwhile, seems totally unaffected by the controversy. He has his own agenda.

The Other Side of the Coin

For all the controversy over Young Jeezy's crack rap status, there's more to his music than just the thug lifestyle. Young Jeezy is often called the "Motivational Rapper." His 2006 album, for instance, *The Inspiration*, is a lot like a coach's speech to his players before the big game. It's intended to be encouraging, inspiring even. Young Jeezy constantly tells the listener to hustle, to work hard, to go out and better themselves however they can. As Young Jeezy himself put it in an interview with MTV:

"I keep telling them, I'm not a rapper, I'm a motivational speaker. I don't do shows, I do seminars."

This vibe within his music has earned him the admiration of many hip-hop reviewers. They give his work titles like "inspirational hip-hop" and "power rap." This attitude, many critics believe, is what's responsible for Young Jeezy's success; he's offering hope and direction to folks who might all too easily give up. He told the *Village Voice*:

"My movement is different. I motivate the thugs. I'm a part of people's everyday rituals that they do. When they get up, they might throw my joint in, and that's how they get their day started before they go out and do whatever it is they got to do. . . . My music is more like ghetto gospel; there's a message in my words, so people listen. Sometimes you might here different things; it depends on how you feel. You might feel down, and I might be the cat in the same sentence saying, 'You need to get up and do your thing.' And then I could be the same cat, when you at the top of your game, telling you, 'It feel good, don't it?' but with the same words. . . . I really talk to people."

Young Jeezy doesn't just rap. He's also participated in actual seminars, meant to inspire people with a better way to do things. In the summer of 2006, Young Jeezy joined a whole slew of other hip-hop figures, including Russell Simmons, at a conference at Morris Brown College. The topic of the conference, called the Hip-Hop Summit, had a lot to do with helping people get ahead by managing their finances wisely. According to the conference description:

> *"The topics to be covered include the basics of banking, home ownership, repairing bad credit and understanding credit scores, entrepreneurship, vehicle financing and more."*

The conference, organized by the Hip-Hop Action Summit Network, was Young Jeezy's way of giving back to his fans. After all, the fans had made his financial success possible, so he wanted to help them get ahead too. As always, he was out to shake people and get them thinking about their lives—and how they could make them better.

Beefs are common in hip-hop, and fortunately most remain verbal. But sometimes the language gets so bad that the song can be released only on mixtapes. No record label would touch it—if they wanted airplay anyway.

Protecting His Neck

Image and substance aren't always exactly the same things. Young Jeezy's image as a thug rapper, for example, isn't what makes him who he is. He's much more complex than that. That complexity comes out not only in his relations with fans, but also in his treatment of one of the mainstays of a hip-hop rapper's career, the beef.

Where's the Beef?

A beef is a hip-hop version of an argument, one that takes the form of rhymes in songs that are meant to insult—or at least annoy—another artist. Often, the artists involved will release entire songs aimed at their rival, even crafting their slam to be so vicious and profane that they'll never be able to make it an official album release, no matter how many *platinum* hits they have. Instead, the chosen medium for a beef is a mixtape, keeping these artists connected to the street. Since mixtapes are generally

Beefs require a talent all their own. A good beef between artists can benefit both their careers.

created without the backing of a major record label, the artist has more freedom to express his feelings in whatever way he wants.

Having a beef with another artist is one route to gaining street cred. Folks admire someone who can lay down a particularly crafty diss rhyme on someone—or come up with a response to a diss that flips it completely around. As such, having a beef or two in hip-hop is popular, and rappers will not only get one for themselves, but also jump into the defense of other artists, based on label or even regional affiliations, creating a huge network of disses and responses to the disses. A hip-hop beef, at it's best, can be a window into the heart of the music, with MCs coming up with tracks far more raw and genuine than anything that ever gets put on an album. At its worst, a hip-hop beef can be the silliest, most juvenile argument imaginable!

The thing with a hip-hop beef, though, is that it's something that never really ends. Any normal argument would probably reach some sort of closure, or at least end with a dead body on the floor. While murder has certainly ended a few beefs in hip-hop, Biggie and Tupac being examples, for the most part, the majority of hip-hop beefing artists are still alive—but although the diss tracks and smack talk may fade for a while, it's a rare thing for anyone to make up. Instead, you get situations like the one between Daddy Yankee and Don Omar, where Daddy refused to appear at a particular music festival once he heard Don Omar would be performing on the same stage.

Jeezy and Beefing

Young Jeezy has had his share of beefs. Most recently, he's had a long series of back-and-forth disses with an artist from Atlanta named Gucci Mane, whom he claims never paid him as promised for appearing on Gucci's hit single "Icy". These sorts of beefs, where rappers take a business matter and use it as material for their music, are fairly common.

In one beef, however, Young Jeezy stands head and shoulders above the rest. Back in the summer of 2005, the famous rapper Nas came out with an album with a controversial title *Hip-Hop Is Dead*. The album insulted current hip-hop stars for not living up to the **genre**, for being ignorant of their roots. From anyone else, this claim might have been brushed off. But Nas had enough cred to make it sting. A whole slew of hip-hop stars, especially those he took swipes at in the songs on *Hip-Hop Is Dead*, instantly jumped on Nas. Critics, producers, and other members of the hip-hop nation also joined the argument.

The response from the stars of the Dirty South and the various subgenres it had spawned was especially angry. Nas slammed Southern hip-hop the most on his CD, clearly pointing his finger at the Southern sound for bringing down the genre. Other hip-hop purists and loyalists had already said the same thing, but not quite so loudly. Anyone who **revered** New York hip-hop's lyrical, heavy poetry dismissed the Dirty South's repetitive dance beats—and lyrics that often contained more grunts than actual rhymes—as the lowest of the low. As a proud representative of the Dirty South, Young Jeezy considered himself dissed (along with all the other rappers from Atlanta to Memphis).

Jeezy chose to respond to Nas on a radio show broadcast out of Philadelphia. He not only denied Nas's "hip-hop is dead" claim, but he also accused Nas of not having street cred. This was certainly typical beef material: one rapper calling the other a poser, and bringing into question the other rapper's ability to be connected to "real" hip-hop. The truly epic beefs of hip-hop had certainly been started for less.

But this beef ultimately turned out to be different. When the press and the critics picked a side in the fight, nearly everyone sided with Nas. After all, Nas was considered a living legend and all-around media darling. Young Jeezy, the media agreed, was an upstart who was simply digging himself a hole by going after the Nasty.

What happened next though is what makes this beef so unique. Jeezy surprised everyone by publicly apologizing only a week later; as a few journalists put it, he "deaded" the beef. In a business where beefs go on as long as there's breath left

Nas ripped Dirty South rap, which includes such talents as Ludacris, on his CD *Hip-Hop Is Dead*. It set off a beef between Nas and Young Jeezy.

in the rappers' bodies, one artist, on his own initiative, actually going on a radio show and apologizing was unheard of. Some people said Jeezy was just afraid of looking like a fool. Many, however, admired Young Jeezy's maturity and humility. Maybe he was just protecting his own neck by refusing to engage in a longstanding beef with one of hip-hop's icons, but Jeezy still stands head and shoulders above the rest when it comes to having the guts to admit he was wrong.

Jeezy told the *Village Voice*:

> *"I ain't arrogant. I don't say things that shouldn't be said. I think before I speak. That's why I don't do the whole beef thing. It's just stupid. Come see me and we'll deal with it. I ain't finna be rapping against you. That's for the birds; that's old-school."*

##

For a self-professed street thug from inner-city Atlanta, Young Jeezy shows he has plenty of character. He wants people to understand that there's more to him than just a cardboard cut-out image of gangsta rapper. He has many more dimensions than that!

He told MVREmix:

> *"Right now I know there's a lot of cats that's hootin' and hollerin', sayin' what they did and what they done. I just don't wanna get caught up in none of that man. You know what I'm sayin'. I'm a real stand up dude. A thorough young [black] man. It's like I don't even wanna get caught up in that. . . . Caught up in that 'He's just a rapper and that's what it is,' 'cause that ain't me. I live life, I do it big. I get that now when I'm out on the road. You know people, they love you*

Nas can beef with the best, and he had no problem responding to Young Jeezy. Of course it didn't hurt that most people in the media sided with Nas.

for who you are but they kind of tend to forget sometimes that you sacrificed a lot to do this and you really been through them trials and trills. I don't want 'em to forget that. I don't want 'em to think 'Ey, it was just all gravy and I'm here now.' Or 'It's all gravy and I'm a rapper now,' I was a real [black man] before this and I'm a be a real [black man] after this."

Young Jeezy deaded the beef between he and Nas, apologizing on a radio program. He says he doesn't want to get caught up in things that detract from the music.

Clearly, Jeezy identifies himself with his roots and with his people. That's who he's all about. And he demonstrates again and again that he's real, not just putting on an act.

When the United States was struck with the greatest natural disaster it had experienced in the past fifty years, for instance, Jeezy stepped forward with a helping hand. He wasn't the only one, of course, but his unique style made his actions particularly powerful.

Tragedy can bring out the best in people. And when the floods hit New Orleans after Hurricane Katrina, hip-hop artists like Young Jeezy proved they had a lot of good in their hearts.

5

Katrina

On August 29, 2005, the City of New Orleans was not a place anyone wanted to be. The city that's home to the Mardi Gras festival, numerous jazz and blues musicians, and both the Cajun and Creole cultures that enriched so much of the Gulf Coast, was a thriving metropolis of nearly a million people—but in the wake of Hurricane Katrina, it turned into a ghost town, thousands of its residents homeless.

The city's lowland was protected by levees—and in the face of Katrina's power, the levees failed. The flood that resulted was the worst natural disaster seen in America in nearly a century. Eighty percent of the city was flooded, with water reaching as high as fifteen feet. All sorts of debris floated in the water: tree branches, bits of building material, motor oil, sewage, beds, chairs, toys, books, and human bodies. Instead of a city, New Orleans became a series of isolated islands in the middle of a toxic sea. Fires couldn't be put out. Looters raided homes, malls, and wherever else they could reach through the muck, and police could do little to stop them. People died of drowning, of injuries, and disease—and emergency services could not get to them. In the Louisiana Superdome, thousands of refugees were trapped, with little in the way of food or medicine, and no working toilets.

Meanwhile, the response to the disaster from both the state and federal governments was lacking. Normally, the Louisiana State National Guard would have been the ones to restore order, but there were simply not enough of them available; most of them had been dispatched to Iraq and Afghanistan months before, along with most of the desperately needed equipment that might have handled the high waters. In the months and years after Katrina, experts tried to make sense out of the disaster. They agreed that the death toll and the millions of dollars of damage was brought about in part by a poor government response.

One area of response that was not poor, however, was the outreach from the general population of the United States. Celebrities took center stage in the fund-raising process, donating money and using their star power to raise even more. In a nationwide telethon to raise money for Katrina, musical artists like hip-hop star Kanye West and rock legend Neil Young took the stage, while other celebrities rewarded people who phoned in donations with one-on-one conversations.

Young Jeezy immediately joined the stream of charity work. Paring up with the Southern crunk star Lil Wayne, he filled several eighteen-wheeler trucks with food, ice, medical supplies, and other necessities and had them shipped to New Orleans. He also took part in several benefit concerts in the Atlanta area.

But Jeezy went even further. He truly put his action where his mouth was and did something no other celebrity did: he took into his own Atlanta home twelve people who had been displaced by Hurricane Katrina. Taking a stranger into your home is a leap of faith and kindness, one that not everyone is willing to make—but Young Jeezy did.

Hip-Hop: Thugs or Philanthropists?

Not everyone is convinced that Jeezy is such a good guy, despite his charitable acts. They believe he has a responsibility to young people, particularly black kids from urban areas, to take a stand against destructive lifestyles. People like Russell Simmons, founder of the Hip-Hop Summit Action Network, believe hip-hop should be a powerful force for good—and that people like Young Jeezy detract from that. According to the network's Web site, the hip-hop world should join together to promote the following goals:

1. *We want freedom and the social, political and economic development and empowerment of our families and communities; and for all women, men and children throughout the world.*

2. *We want equal justice for all without discrimination based on race, color, ethnicity, nationality, gender, sexual orientation, age, creed or class.*

3. *We want the total elimination of poverty.*

4. *We want the highest quality public education equally for all.*

Entire neighborhoods were devastated by the floodwaters. When relief was slow to arrive, Young Jeezy and Lil Wayne did what they could to get relief to the people.

5. *We want the total elimination of racism and racial profiling, violence, hatred and bigotry.*

6. *We want universal access and delivery of the highest quality health care for all.*

7. *We want the total elimination of police brutality and the unjust incarceration of people of color and all others.*

8. *We want the end and repeal of all repressive legislations, laws, regulations and ordinances such as 'three strikes' laws; federal and state mandatory minimum sentencing; trying and sentencing juveniles as adults; sentencing disparities between crack and powdered cocaine use; capitol punishment; the Media Marketing Accountability Act; and hip-hop censorship fines by the FCC.*

9. *We want reparations to help repair the lingering vestiges; damages and suffering of African Americans as a result of the brutal enslavement of generations of Africans in America.*

10. *We want the progressive transformation of American society into a Nu America as a result of organizing and mobilizing the energy, activism and resources of the hip-hop community at the grass-roots level throughout the United States.*

11. *We want greater unity, mutual dialogue, program development and a prioritizing of national issues for collective action within the hip-hop community through summits, conferences, workshops, issue task force and joint projects.*

12. *We want advocacy of public policies that are in the interests of hip-hop before Congress, state legislatures, municipal governments, the media and the entertainment industry.*

13. *We want the recertification and restoration of voting rights for the 10 million persons who have loss their right to vote as a result of a felony conviction. Although these persons have served time in prison, their voting rights have not been restored in 40 states in the U.S.*

14. *We want to tremendously increase public awareness and education on the pandemic of HIV/AIDS.*

15. *Communities in which poor and minorities reside being deliberately targeted for toxic waste dumps, facilities and other environmental hazards."*

These are pretty lofty goals compared to Jeezy's simple philosophy of hustling. All he really wants is to help people get ahead.

But whatever else you think about him, Jeezy does take seriously his power as a voice for his people. He uses his talents to make himself rich, but he also uses them to encourage and motivate others. When UnderGroundOnline asked him what inspired his album *Thug Motivation*, he replied:

"Definitely the streets, just knowing how hard it is on the streets. Just knowing that people were there just waiting to hear. I wanted to let fans know that they were not there by themselves, that they were not alone and that I miss them."

Russell Simmons is a business mogul and an icon in the hip-hop world. He believes that hip-hop has the power to do good and to make powerful changes in the world.

According to Young Jeezy, people, especially young people, need to be motivated to do something better with their lives. He hopes his music helps kids to find a life off the streets.

Jeezy also told the *Village Voice*:

"At the end of the day, it's still good music. There's a message, and everybody from working people to corporate people to college people to street people, we all speak the same language. It's like a translation for the people who really don't know about the life, I translate it for them, make them understand why certain people do certain things. . . . It's basically saying, 'Look this is what it is.' Even with the kids, that's why a lot of people don't really trip on the kids. That's reality, that's what really happens, so why would you hide it from them? I take it as they listen to the music and then say, 'I didn't know it was really like that out there. I might don't wanna be out there. I might want to go to school so I can go to college because that ain't what I want to go through.' And then for the people that's out there, that's going, '. . .you right, maybe I should step my game up. I been content for a long time; maybe it's time to go for mine.' There's people in the corporate world that got good jobs with drug habits and [stuff]. But at the end of the day, if they got someone telling them, 'Hey man, [forget] that, let's get money,' that might be a good reason for them to be like, '. . . I'm a get money and worry about that other [stuff] later on.' People who are sitting right now in the projects going, '. . .I might can't go buy a three million-dollar mansion, but I can get my family up out of here and get us a nice house that's comfortable for us until everything else work out,' at least give them that inspiration and motivation to want to do that instead of just being content, being like, 'This is life, that's how it is, it's going to be like that because ain't nobody tell me no different.' You have people that stay in they hoods all they life and don't go nowhere

Young Jeezy has worked hard for what he's achieved, and he believes that others can do the same. They might not be hip-hop stars, but people can set and achieve constructive goals. He hopes that his music provides them with inspiration and motivation.

else. But you get a cat like me that been to [pretty] near every hood in the world and got down with the best in the city telling you."

When it comes right down to it, some would say what Jeezy's doing is speaking the truth—and that ultimately, it's the truth that sets us all free.

1973   Hip-hop begins in the rec room of Kool Herc.

Sept. 28,
1979   Jay Jenkins, the future Young Jeezy, is born in Columbia, South Carolina.

2001   Young Jeezy releases his first album.

2003   *Come Shop wit Me* is released.

2005   Young Jeezy joins Boyz n Da Hood, and its first album is released.

2005   Young Jeezy's *Let's Get It: Thug Motivation 101* is released.

2005   Young Jeezy puts out a line of t-shirts.

2005   Young Jeezy gets in a beef with Nas.

2005   Young Jeezy participates in several projects for Hurricane Katrina relief efforts; he also brings some of the hurricane's homeless into his Atlanta home.

Oct.
2005   Young Jeezy leaves Boyz n Da Hood.

2006 Young Jeezy is named New York's King of Hip-Hop by *XXL* magazine.

2006 Young Jeezy expands his clothing line.

2006 *The Inspiration* is released.

2006 Young Jeezy participates in the Hip-Hop Summit.

Albums

2001 *Thuggin Under the Influence*

2003 *Come Shop wit Me*

2005 *Let's Get It: Thug Motivation*

2006 *The Inspiration*

Number-One Singles

2005 "Soul Survivor" (with Akon)

DVDs

2005 *Hoodz, Vol. 4: Young Jeezy*

2006 *Cornbread Presents: Young Jeezy, Vol. 1*

2006 *Young Jeezy: Thug Motivation*

Awards/Recognition

2006 *XXL* magazine: Names Young Jeezy New York's King of Hip-Hop.

Books

Bogdanov, Vladimir, Chris Woodstra, Steven Thomas Erlewine, and John Bush (eds.). All Music Guide to Hip-Hop: The Definitive Guide to Rap and Hip-Hop. San Francisco, Calif.: Backbeat Books, 2003.

Chang, Jeff. Can't Stop Won't Stop: A History of the Hip-Hop Generation. New York: Picador, 2005.

Emcee Escher and Alex Rappaport. The Rapper's Handbook: A Guide to Freestyling, Writing Rhymes, and Battling. New York: Flocabulary Press, 2006.

George, Nelson. Hip Hop America. New York: Penguin, 2005.

Kusek, Dave, and Gerd Leonhard. The Future of Music: Manifesto for the Digital Music Revolution. Boston, Mass.: Berkley Press, 2005.

Light, Alan (ed.). The Vibe History of Hip Hop. New York: Three Rivers Press, 1999.

Waters, Rosa. Hip-Hop: A Short History. Broomall, Pa.: Mason Crest, 2007.

Watkins, S. Craig. Hip Hop Matters: Politics, Pop Culture, and the Struggle for the Soul of a Movement. Boston, Mass.: Beacon Press, 2006.

Web Sites

Corporate Thugz Entertainment
www.youngjeezy.com

Young Jeezy on Def Jam
www.defjam.com/site/artist_home.php?artist_id=567

Young Jeezy on MySpace
www.myspace.com/youngjeezy

Glossary

controversial—Causing disagreement.

credibility—Believability.

culture—The beliefs, customs, practices, and social behavior of a particular nation or people.

entrepreneur—Someone who sets up and finances new business enterprises to make a profit.

genre—A category into which a work of art can be placed based on its style, medium, and subject.

mixtapes—A compilation of songs recorded from other sources.

moguls—Important or powerful people.

platinum—A designation indicating that a recording has sold one million units.

rap—A music style characterized by spoken rhyming vocals and often featuring a looped electronic beat in the background.

revered—Treated someone with admiration and deep respect.

tracks—A separate piece of music on a disk, tape, or record.

Index

50 Cent 27, 29

beefs 34, 35–42
Boyz n Da Hood 19, 20

Come Shop wit Me (album) 19
Corporate Thugz Entertainment 18

Daddy Yankee 37
DJ Kool Herc 10
Don Omar 37
drugs 16, 17, 18, 28, 30, 31, 53

East Coast 10, 12, 13

Hip-Hop is Dead (album) 38–39
Hip-Hop Summit Action Network 47
Hurricane Katrina 44, 45–47, 49, 51, 53, 55

Inspiration, The (album) 20, 31

Jay-Z 10, 11, 23

"King of Hip-Hop" 8, 10

Lil Jon 9
Lil Wayne 13, 46, 48
Ludacris 39

Mane, Gucci 37
mixtape 12, 23, 34, 35

Nas 10, 38–39, 41, 42
New York City 8, 9, 10, 11, 13, 15, 36, 38
Notorious B.I.G 10, 16

P Diddy 23

Shakur, Tupac 12, 16, 28, 37
Simmons, Russell 30, 32, 47, 51
Snowman, the 20–22
southern rap 9, 10, 12, 13, 16, 23
    Dirty South 10, 12, 38–39

Thuggin Under the Influence (album) 18
Thug Motivation 101 (album) 9, 19
T.I. 9

violence 22, 24, 26, 28, 29, 30, 31, 44

West Coast, 10, 12, 13
Wu-Tang Clan 16

Young Jeezy
    beef 35–43
    clothing line 20–22, 23
    drugs and violence 28,
        30–31
    early music 16, 18–20
    gangsta 28

Hurricane Katrina 44–
    47, 48
hustling 18, 28
inspiration 24–25, 31–33,
    50–55
mixtapes 23
Southern rapper 10, 12, 13
youth 14–16
*Young Jeezy Presents
U.S.D.A* (mixtape) 23

About the Author

Nat Cotts would be called a backpack boy by anyone who was truly in the business of hip-hop. He still listens to the current hits and enjoys writing about the music.

Picture Credits

Flickr
    brookenovak- cc-att-sa 2.0: p. 18
    DJSemtex- cc-att-sa 2.0: p. 42
istockphotos: p. 52
    Bergmann, Dean: p. 14
    Brunt, Christa: p. 17
    Edwards, Jeremy: p. 8
    Machhaus, Tobias: p. 34
    Newman, Stacey: p. 24
    Nickischer, Joseph: p. 44
    O'Claire, Sandra: p. 48
    O'Driscoll, Christopher: p 25
    steps: p. 21
    Vanovitch, Lisa: p. 30
    Welles, Katherine: p. 12
    Zhenikeyev, Arman: p. 36
PR Photos: p. 41
    Bielawski, Adam: p. 39
    Graffiti Press: p. 29
    Hatcher, Chris: p. 11
    Mayer Janet: p. 51
    Thompson, Terry: front cover, p. 2, 54

To the best knowledge of the publisher, all other images are in the public domain. If any image has been inadvertently uncredited, please notify Harding House Publishing Service, Vestal, New York 13850, so that rectification can be made for future printings.